Hummingbirds

Leo Statts

abdopublishing.com

Published by Abdo Zoom, a division of ABDO, P.O. Box 398166, Minneapolis, Minnesota 55439.

Copyright © 2018 by Abdo Consulting Group, Inc. International copyrights reserved in all countries.

No part of this book may be reproduced in any form without written permission from the publisher.

Printed in the United States of America, North Mankato, Minnesota.

092017

012018

THIS BOOK CONTAINS
RECYCLED MATERIALS

Photo Credits: iStock, Shutterstock

Production Contributors: Kenny Abdo, Jennie Forsberg, Grace Hansen, John Hansen

Design Contributors: Dorothy Toth, Neil Klinepier

Publisher's Cataloging-in-Publication Data

Names: Statts, Leo, author.

Title: Hummingbirds / by Leo Statts.

Description: Minneapolis, Minnesota: Abdo Zoom, 2018. | Series: Awesome birds |
   Includes online resource and index.

Identifiers: LCCN 2017939222 | ISBN 9781532120596 (lib.bdg.) | ISBN 9781532121715 (ebook) |
   ISBN 9781532122279 (Read-to-Me ebook)

Subjects: LCSH: Hummingbirds--Juvenile literature. | Birds--Juvenile literature.

Classification: DDC 598.7/64--dc23

LC record available at https://lccn.loc.gov/2017939222

Table of Contents

Hummingbirds

There are more than 300 different types of hummingbird species.

They are known for their flying skills.

Body

Hummingbirds are small and brightly colored. Males are more colorful than females.

Their throats can be brightly colored.

Habitat

Hummingbirds live in both North and South America. They can be found in many **habitats**, like rain forests and deserts.

Most live in warm places with flowers.

Some live in cold places. They **migrate** to warmer areas each winter.

Food

Hummingbirds are **omnivores**.

They eat small insects. They also eat **nectar**.

Some people put up feeders with sugar water in them. This attracts the hummingbirds.

Female hummingbirds lay two eggs at a time. They sit on the eggs to keep them warm.

Hummingbirds live only a few years. They can live up to 3 or 4 years.

Average Length

A hummingbird is longer than a baseball.

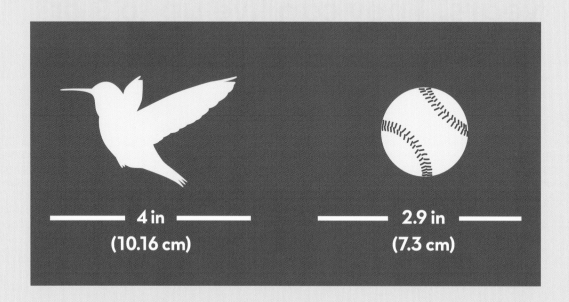

4 in
(10.16 cm)

2.9 in
(7.3 cm)

Quick Stats

Average Weight

A hummingbird is heavier than a quarter.

0.3 oz
(8.5 g)

0.16 oz
(4.53 g)

Glossary

habitat – a place where a living thing is naturally found.

migrate – to move from one place to another, often to find food or water.

nectar – a sweet liquid, or sugar water, that flowering plants make.

omnivore – an animal that eats both plants and animals.

species – living things that are very much alike.

Online Resources

For more information on hummingbirds, please visit **abdobooklinks.com**

Learn even more with the Abdo Zoom Animals database. Visit **abdozoom.com** today!

Index